BLAZING A TRAIL:
The Unconventional Life
of Harriet Hosmer

Harriet Hosmer, circa 1850

"Nothing could conceal that inner fire of the spirit, that glowing light of genius…" *

*Cornelia, Carr, Letters & Memories, 239
Photo used with permission of the Watertown Free Public Library, Watertown, Mass.

BLAZING A TRAIL:
The Unconventional Life
of Harriet Hosmer

Barbara Kailean Welsh

FIRST EDITION
Spirit Time Press
Viroqua, WI

Blazing A Trail:
The Unconventional Life of Harriet Hosmer

Copyright © 2017 by Barbara Kailean Welsh

ISBN: 978-09990289-0-2

The author made good faith effort to ensure the accuracy and completeness of information contained in this book. Any errors, omissions or derogatory impressions of the people, places or events portrayed herein are unintentional.

With appreciation to the following for their expertise and professional support:
Deb Paulson, Zelda Productions, Decorah, Iowa, cover and book design
Ellen Modersohn, Lansing, Iowa, editing
Betsy Stahl, Lansing, Iowa, photographs
Johnson's Printing, Rochester, Minnesota

To order additional copies, please contact us.

SPIRIT TIME PRESS
373 W South St
Viroqua, WI 54665
608-638-0005
support@kaileanwelsh.com

♥

This book is dedicated to all men and women
who have the strength to step off the beaten path
when they feel their walk lies on another.

With special thoughts of my parents,
William and Esther Welsh,
and my dear brother, Greg,
who through acceptance, courage, and
conviction showed me the importance
of walking the path that was right for me.

To my sisters, Janice, Jean, Rose, and Mary, who hold me steady
and help me up when I falter, and
my brothers, Gary and Mike, who always have my back.

And to my mentors and friends
in the Global Association of Holistic Psychotherapy (the GAHP)
who helped me find my voice and who keep me moving forward.

TABLE OF CONTENTS

✳

Author's Note

arriet Hosmer intrigued me from the start. When
I heard the story of how the local river bluff was
named for her and that she had gone on to become a
famous sculptor, I wanted to know more.

Over the years, I've come to know a fascinating woman,
with a richness and depth to her nature that was uncommon
in her time, and is still so today. Not many people step out of
prescribed roles, social conventions, and limiting beliefs about
what is possible, to follow their dreams and live their passions,
yet that is what Harriet did. She allowed herself a bigger vision.

Mentored and encouraged by strong, independent women
she met along the way, Harriet believed that women had "the
God-given right to follow any calling for which they had the
ability. To be an actress, writer, musician, painter, poet, even
astronomer....was possible for a woman willing to study, work
hard, endure ridicule, and step over the stumbling blocks in her
path."[1]

In a time when women "had their place," like children who were to be seen and not heard, Harriet made herself heard. She once said that all that holds people back is the illusion of their inadequacies, "created by a mind unwilling to confront its own vast potential."[2]

Harriet Hosmer didn't hold back. From birth to death, she challenged nineteenth century expectations of women, unwilling to accept anything less than full expression of the gifts she was given. She lived her truth, and she lived life to capacity.

Harriet's life took her from the depths of loss to the heights of professional acclaim. She did work that she loved. She hung out with the rich and famous—kings and queens, authors, poets, and artists—whose names and works live on across time. She had deep and meaningful friendships that spanned decades. She laughed and played. Described by her friend Matilda Hayes as "the happiest human being that I know," Harriet Hosmer was "universally respected and, where known, loved."[3]

Despite a tragic childhood, or maybe because of it, Harriet learned to do life well. She was confident, curious, and genuine, with an enthusiastic desire to take in all life had to offer. She chose to see the good, living with a strong faith that a greater force worked in her life. "We are assured," she said, "and it is this belief which throws sunshine over the darkest shadows of life, that however inexplicable to us are sometimes the decrees of Providence, they are forever wise and just and merciful, and that sooner or later we shall have wisdom to acknowledge them as blessings."[4]

Her motto was simple: "Live well, do well, and all will be well."[5]

Harriet Hosmer did well. Her life had an impact–on the art world, on social thought, on the hearts of those she touched in friendship, and, not least of all, on a rugged Mississippi bluff in a tiny town in the corner of northeast Iowa.

I noticed as I was writing this that my name for Harriet changed at different stages of her story. She is Hatty during her rambunctious childhood and adventurous young adulthood. When she finished her education, stepped forward into the world independently, and moved to Rome as an eager young artist, she became Harriet. Occasionally, I refer to her as Miss Hosmer–the successful and mature woman. And every once in a while, in the fullness of her being, she is Harriet Hosmer, strong in her truth and steady in her personal power. She was never Hosmer; none of her relationships were ever that impersonal.

Harriet spoke once about how fun it would be "to come back to this earth after having been a wandering ghost for a hundred years or so and see what has been going on in flesh" while she had been "going on in spirit."[6] If she could be around, I'd like to think we'd be good friends.

I hope you enjoy getting to know Harriet Hosmer as much as I have.

Barbara Kailean Welsh

---

[1] Dolly Sherwood, *Harriet Hosmer: American Sculptor 1830-1908* (Chicago:University of Chicago Press, 1991), 22.

[2] Charles Colbert, "Harriet Hosmer & Spiritualism." *American Art* 10, 3 (1996), 46

[3] Cornelia Carr, ed., *Harriet Hosmer Letters and Memories* (New York: Moffat, Yard and Company, 1912, reprint), 69.

[4] Ibid, 186.

[5] Sherwood, 52, Carr, 19.

[6] Sherwood, 329.

PROLOGUE

Hatty was never one to back away from a challenge, and this day was no exception. As the steamboat the *Senator*, with Hatty aboard, approached the little Mississippi River port of Lansing, Iowa, the towering riverbluff beckoned.

The stories vary a bit, but the most popular version tells of a race to the summit. It is said that some young male passengers pointed to the prominent hillside and, derisively judging feminine physical ability, declared that Hatty would never be able to beat them to the top.

They obviously didn't know her well. The twenty-year-old was a strong athlete and fierce competitor, eager to show off the physical strength she developed from years of outdoor play as a child. Hatty boldly responded. Wagers were made, and up the 450-foot hillside they raced.

First to the top, the vivacious young woman forever left her mark on the developing little river town. Previously unnamed, the towering limestone bluff was that day christened in her honor, Mount Hosmer.

Now, it is most unusual for a place to be named for someone many years before they become famous. But Mount Hosmer is one of those rare places, and there was nothing usual about Harriet Hosmer.

The race that day was a simple random event of youth. No one present knew that Hatty, or Harriet Goodhue Hosmer, as she was formally named, would go on to become famous across the continents, blazing trails where most women dared not tread. Defying the limitations and gender expectations of her time, she became American's most famous woman sculptor of the 19th century, achieving international recognition and breaking down social and professional barriers to allow freedom for women in ways never before experienced.

The physical prowess and determination that took Harriet Hosmer to the top of the river bluff were crucial to her eventual fame and success. From solid blocks of marble, her strong young arms would chisel exquisite shapes. Through an art form previously entrusted only to men, she would carve success.

Those who knew Harriet during her lifetime considered themselves blessed, touched by her zest for living, her deep and loyal friendship, and her visionary spirit. To art historians, she remains legendary. But despite a lifetime of accomplishments and notoriety, with her work still exhibited in the world's best museums, Harriet Hosmer is once again largely unknown. Most visitors to the Mississippi river bluff that carries her name know little about the pioneering artist and her visionary spirit.

Harriet Goodhue Hosmer
1830-1908

"Still better than being a great artist it will be, to be great as a human being."

1

※

CHILDHOOD: TRAGEDY & INDEPENDENCE

Harriet's Hosmer's life was never typical. Her childhood was a unique blend of tragedy and loneliness, boldness and color. She was born October 9, 1830, in Watertown, Massachusetts, near Boston, the second child of Hiram and Sarah (Grant) Hosmer. Death repeatedly marked her early years. When she was just two years old, her baby brother, Hiram, died after living only two months. Within a year, brother George was born, but he died too, just before his second birthday.

A form of infantile tuberculosis was said to be the reason for both of their deaths. Tuberculosis or "consumption," as it was called then, was one of the most prevalent and insidious diseases of the time. In May 1836, as lilacs and wood violets bloomed in Watertown, it struck the family a third time, claiming Harriet's mother Sarah, at age 33. Hatty was only five years old, her sister Sarah Helen just two years older.

Harriet rarely mentioned her mother again, often diverting the conversation when asked about her tragic losses. A glimpse of her pain is clear in words she wrote at age 18 to her friend Cornelia Carr, whose younger sister had died. Harriet acknowledged her friend's loss and wrote of her mother: "Nothing can supply her place…no love can be so strong, no influence so great."[1]

Harriet's father, a Harvard graduate and distinguished physician, was determined that the little bodies of his motherless daughters would be made strong and sturdy enough to ward off any predisposition to tuberculosis they might have. Contrary to the social norms of the time in which pale was fashionable and girls were typically cosseted and protected, Hiram encouraged his daughters to spend much of their day in rigorous outdoor activity. It was a life in which Hatty thrived. Sadly, Sarah Helen did not. She died on Independence Day, 1842, not yet 14-years-old, of the same disease that had claimed her mother and brothers. Her grave joined those of her family already in Mount Auburn Cemetery, Cambridge, Massachusetts.

Neighbors remembered Hatty as "a round-faced, dimpled child, holding a black dog that she had rigged up in red ribbons and bells."[2] At twelve, she became an independent young explorer. A notorious tomboy, she roamed the neighborhood with a skulking yellow cat and a gun for protection. Hatty climbed trees, shot both gun and bow and arrow with precision, and rode her horse fearlessly, sometimes "standing on it as she tore through the streets of Watertown."[3]

The Hosmer home sat on an embankment high above the Charles River, offering Hatty ample opportunity for rowing and swimming in the summer and skating in the winter. She spent many hours playing at the river, watching fishermen pull in their nets filled with shad. Her father had a gondola built for her, with a silver prow and velvet cushions. It was quite the envy of the neighborhood, though "her companions were terrified of riding in it with the daredevil Hatty as gondolier."[4]

Along the natural overhang of the riverbank, Hatty created her first studio, modeling in clay surrounded by a collection of specimens: frogs, rats, birds, snakes—both death and alive. A young playmate recalled Hatty, in her smock, brandishing a small ivory handgun tipped with silver. She had once used it to shoot a robin that she needed to examine, "just to get it right."[5] In her father's office was a skeleton that Hatty often dressed in her cousin Alfred's borrowed clothes, as most other girls would dress a doll. She was always eager to learn and she used the environment around her to do so.

It was a free and simple life for young Hatty, one that fostered a love for the beauty and majesty in nature. "For miles around, there was no wildwood path she hadn't explored…no shady cove where her boat hadn't rested, and in her search for mosses and wildflowers, no neighboring hillside left unclimbed."[6]

Although those who knew her well found her appealing," many in Watertown thought Hatty peculiar.[7] Most likely, she would have agreed. She joked with her father, "The Hosmers are the most crooked sticks that God or the Devil ever concocted."[8] She also insisted that she was descended from the powerful Norse God, Odin.

Hattie did not do well with formal education. It was difficult for her to give up outdoor delights for the indoor structure of the classroom. Her school attendance was sporadic, and as she approached adolescence, she was often reprimanded for insolence and misbehavior. She was expelled three times, on one occasion labeled a miscreant after making guttural, dissonant, nonsense sounds while practicing for a choral event.[9] Hatty later recalled "the long explanatory note attached to my back when I was sent home in disgrace."[10]

With each expulsion, Dr. Hosmer became more convinced that a highly structured classroom was too confining for his daughter. Governesses and tutors filled the gaps and Hatty again ran free.

Her antics became more colorful, outrageous, and dangerous. One night she rode the twenty-mile round trip to Boston alone just to satisfy a bet. Another time she put a counterfeit bill in the church collection. At the height of her mischief, she thought it would be fun to uncouple the railroad cars from the engine so that the passengers would be left behind. She was apprehended just before the climactic moment and bailed out by her father, who paid for the damages.[11]

People certainly noticed Hatty's antics, but no one seemed to notice her deep loneliness, and how "keenly she longed for…. the ties of family life and love."[12]

At age 15, Hatty's escapades hit a new high when she sent false information to a Boston newspaper reporting the death of Dr. Eliakim Morse, a wealthy, ancient Watertown character, who lived as a legend in his palatial mansion. Hatty secretly watched in amusement as friends and neighbors came to express their condolences. The incident set off a community uproar.[13] Neighbors sympathized with poor Dr. Hosmer, for the losses he'd had to bear, and for the difficulty of trying to manage such a rambunctious child. Even though her father indulged her, he stressed to Harriet the importance of "establishing a character, a good character, without which life is certainly a failure."[14]

Hiram Hosmer, knew his daughter's unbridled freedom and zest for living needed to be contained. Hatty knew it too. She later acknowledged that a change was necessary "for the greater tranquility of the town."[15]

---

[1] Culkin, Kate: *Harriet Hosmer: A Cultural Biography.* (University of Massachusetts Press, 2010), 8.

[2] Sherwood, *Harriet Hosmer,* 12.

[3] "The Hosmer Family, *History Begins at Home: Stories of Watertown*, http://www.watertown.k12.ma.us (accessed April 16, 2017).

[4] Sherwood, p. 12.

[5] Ibid.

[6] Carr, Cornelia: *Harriet Hosmer: Letters and Memories*, 2.

[7] Sherwood, 12.

[8] Ibid, 8.

[9] Ibid, 14.

[10] Ibid, 13.

[11] Ibid, 14.

[12] Ibid, 120.

[13] Ibid, 12.

[14] Carr, *Harriet Hosmer: L&M*, 8.

[15] "Harriet Hosmer in her Native Town." *New York Times*, September 23, 1895.

2

✳

MRS. SEDGWICK'S SCHOOL FOR GIRLS

When Hatty turned 16 years old, her father sent her to Mrs. Charles Sedgwick's School for Girls in Lenox, Massachusetts. Elizabeth Sedgwick, who ran the private academy, was a progressive educator and a woman of great warmth and keen intelligence. She told Dr. Hosmer, "I have the reputation of knowing how to train wild colts, and I will try this one."[1]

Mrs. Sedgwick later described Hatty as "the most difficult pupil to manage that I ever saw, but I think I never saw one in whom I took so deep an interest and whom I learned to love so well."[2]

The great natural beauty of the Berkshires, with pine forests, cold running streams, and mirror-like lakes, was a perfect setting for Hatty. The school's spacious and comfortable home, lovingly called The Hive for its constant activity, offered healthy freedom, motherly care, and cultural opportunities with some of the most creative minds of the day. Elizabeth Sedgwick took the education of the female mind seriously and strove to create an environment that was intellectually stimulating, requiring students to think and analyze for themselves.

Hatty's rambunctiousness was seen as high-spirited and good humored. She brought the house to life, with her stories, improvisations, and daring escapades. "We all laughed immoderately at nothing," a friend wrote of their time together, "as people always do when Hattie Hosmer is present."[3]

But Hatty also embodied a serious side that appealed to older people as well as to the other girls. "Already the mingling of the grave and the gay in her temperament made her wonderfully attractive to minds of varied tone and of diverse ages," her dear friend Cornelia Crow Carr, later wrote.[4]

Harriet developed a great friendship with Cornelia, who became her "chosen classmate, confidante, and sister mine."[5] Harriet and Cornelia talked about their desire to leave their mark on the world. That they could be so open about their ambitions is evidence of the school's progressive atmosphere in an era when all women of their class were discouraged not only from working, but even from appearing in public unescorted. Cultural constraints on women in America were beginning to be challenged and Mrs. Sedgwick's School for Girls encouraged free-thinking. The school was said to offer an atmosphere where feminism "did not have to be articulated; it was inbred."[6]

Harriet embraced this welcoming community of women. She became friends with the celebrated English actress Frances Anne Kemble, who was a neighbor and frequent guest, and Miss Catherine M. Sedgwick, Charles' sister and America's foremost authoress. A steady stream of visiting literary figures enriched the atmosphere of the schoolroom. Among them were authors Ralph Waldo Emerson, Nathaniel Hawthorne, Herman Melville, Oliver Wendell Holmes, and Henry Wadsworth Longfellow.[7] The school's liberal ambience also drew progressive women. Early feminists such as Fredericka Stone, a Unitarian who spoke out for abolition and suffrage, were among those who came to speak.

Hatty's three years at Lenox were a turning point in her life. At Mrs. Sedgwick's, the lonely young girl was accepted and nurtured, "finally finding a salve for the pain of her early losses."[8] Hatty would leave with the belief that she could achieve any dream, as long as she took responsibility for her own learning and looked inward for her gifts and talents.[9]

Though her behavior became less troublesome and disruptive at Mrs. Sedgwick's, Harriet continued to seek education and adventure. On one occasion, she panicked onlookers as she climbed to the top of a 40-foot-high tree to retrieve a crow's nest for study. She maintained her individuality and her spontaneity, even as she grew more responsible and mature.

Just as her father had hoped, Harriet developed a strong and independent character. A *New York Times* article described her as a person "whose magic touch compels things to happen, whether or not they are possible."[10]

[1] Culkin, Kate: *Harriet Hosmer: A Cultural Biography,* 10.

[3] Sherwood, 21.

[3] Culkin, 63.

[4] Carr, *Harriet Hosmer: L&M,* 3.

[5] Sherwood, 18.

[6] Ibid.

[7] Jane Backstrom, "Harriet Hosmer, Feminist Sculptor," *Houston Peace News,* (February 1994), 3.

[8] Culkin, 10.

[9] Ibid.

[10] "Woman as Artist: A Biography of Harriet Hosmer, Our First Woman Sculptor," *New York Times,* July 14, 1912.

3

✳

BREAKING DOWN BARRIERS:
ANATOMY STUDIES

In the fall of 1849, at age 19, Hatty returned to Watertown. She had a new sense of purpose, was clear in her desire to be a sculptor, and was ready to get to work. Hatty and her father had an understanding that sculpture was to be a profession, not a polite, pretty hobby. She must not be satisfied with carving ivory umbrella handles or cutting cameos. So she began her studies in modeling and drawing with Peter Stephenson, an English-born sculptor teaching in Boston.

Hatty and Dr. Hosmer knew that a thorough understanding of anatomy would be crucial to her success, but barriers quickly arose. No college in New England would allow a female to study human anatomy. It was an era when women had "limbs" not "legs" and Harriet's request shocked those in charge at the

Boston Medical Society. The prospect of a woman attending medical school was unacceptable. Opponents argued that women were too refined and delicate to discuss the unsavory aspects of disease. Exposing them to the grisly task of dissecting bodies was unthinkable, especially in coed classrooms."[1] Harriet's request was seen as a "gross impropriety"—it was "not a woman's place to inquire as to the structure of the human frame."[2]

Harriet persisted. A year later, in the fall of 1850, she traveled to St. Louis and sought the help of one of its leading citizens, Cornelia's father, Wayman Crow. The prominent businessman and state legislator became a key figure in Harriet's life. She often turned to him for guidance and he was one of her most ardent supporters and generous benefactors. Their close alliance, evident in their correspondence, continued until Crow's death in 1885, when Harriet spoke sadly of the loss of "the dear Pater."[3]

Mr. Crow used his influence to persuade Dr. Joseph Nash McDowell, the head of the medical department of the state university of Missouri, popularly called McDowell's Medical College, to give Hatty a chance to learn. A brilliant doctor and teacher, McDowell was also legendary for his "eccentricity and whimsy."[4] Hatty recalled McDowell telling her she got into the program, assuring her that "if anybody attempted to interfere with her, he would have to walk over my dead body first."[5] McDowell later expressed great pride in being the one who gave the eager young sculptor her start.

Hatty never missed a session at the college, even through

the harsh winter. Each morning she walked nearly two miles to the school, wearing the brown bonnet that would become her trademark. She went to Professor McDowell's library, where she was allowed to study an abstract of the lecture he had prepared for his male students that day and examine any specimens used to demonstrate the lesson. She spent afternoons and evenings studying, and when the five-month term ended, she received a certificate of proficiency.

As would be the pattern for many of her relationships, Hatty developed a strong bond with Dr. McDowell. After she left St. Louis, the professor sent a message of farewell to his dear student: "The bench you sat upon has never been filled since you were there. I often turn to the spot and I think I can see the little Quaker girl in the brown sacque and close fitting bonnet, and an eye that beamed with pleasure at the exhibition of Nature and Nature's work."[6]

---

[1] Culkin, 15.

[2] Sherwood, 23.

[3] Ibid, 323.

[4] Ibid, 24.

[5] Ibid, 23.

[6] Ibid, 19.

"I become more and more convinced that the place where one is born is the only place one can really love."

4

✳

Traveling the Mississippi

In St. Louis, Hatty felt a strong pull to the Father of Waters, the Mississippi River. Like the Charles River of her youth, the mighty Mississippi offered a path for adventure and she was eager to explore.

To celebrate her graduation, in the early spring of 1851, Hatty set out for New Orleans with Cornelia. The trip quickly became a challenge as the boat they traveled on repeatedly went aground on the swiftly shifting sandbars. Impatient with their progress, Cornelia caught a northbound ship and returned home. Hatty persisted, her boat towed through the graveyard of stranded boats to continue downriver to New Orleans, where she delighted in the quaint old French town before returning to St. Louis.

Hatty marveled that the Mississippi could be "so long and so wide–and apparently made expressly for America."[1] Enamored, she continued northward, determined to explore the Upper Mississippi, the portion of the river she later declared the most beautiful.

Hatty felt called by the deep wilderness and rich history in this section of the country. Land settlement of the area was in its early stages and towns were just beginning to develop. It was a primeval wilderness, a rugged terrain with sandstone bluffs, wide prairies, and dense forests, where buckskin clad explorers and fur trappers camped and Native Americans lived along the riverbanks. Fascinated by the high bluffs that rimmed the river, Hatty was mesmerized by the untamed beauty. She wrote of her journey: "As the paddleboat traveled northward, the water of the Mississippi turned a deep green, with majestic cliffs and crenellated castles of rock rising above the shimmering river on either side."[2]

The French writer, Alexis de Toqueville, had summed up the magnificence of the Upper Mississippi a few years earlier: "All things considered, the valley of the Mississippi is the most magnificent habitation ever prepared by God for man."[3]

Mark Twain, in his book, *Life on the Mississippi,* agreed, writing, "It's all as tranquil and reposeful as dreamland."[4]

Hatty was a passenger on the steamboat, the *Senator,* piloted by the well-known Captain Orrin Smith. The *Senator* was the only boat regularly running the 660-mile trip between St. Louis and St. Paul.

True to her curious nature, Hatty made the most of her travels. She spent hours in the pilothouse talking with

Captain Smith, learning all she could about the river and her surroundings. She accepted an invitation to join a group touring a lead mine in Dubuque, Iowa, where they descended into the mine, transported one-by-one to its depths in a bucket.[5] Hatty later said she almost lost her life when the bucket tipped and threatened to throw her into the dark void. Panicked, she thought about how far she was from home and wondered how those who loved her would know her whereabouts.[6] She met "Indian braves and squaws" at encampments along the shore and smoked "the Pipe of Peace" with at least one Dakota chief.[7]

Hatty's river travels took her to the Mississippi's upper navigable limits, near the then tiny village of St. Paul. She disembarked to see the Falls of St. Anthony, referring to their beauty as sublime,[8] the word used in the nineteenth century for sites that inspired ultimate awe and wonder. Hatty would continuously seek those qualities throughout her lifetime.

---

[1] Sherwood, 31.

[2] Ibid.

[3] William J. Burke, *The Upper Mississippi Valley*, Mississippi Valley Press, 2000, 155.

[4] Mark Twain, *Life on the Mississippi*

[5] Sherwood, 31.

[6] Ibid.

[7] Carr, HH L&M, 11.

[8] Sherwood, p. 32

"We are assured that however inexplicable the decrees of Providence, sooner or later we shall have wisdom to acknowledge them as blessings."

5

✳

THE NAMING OF
MOUNT HOSMER

A s the *Senator* followed its northward path, it
approached the small settlement of Lansing in the
northeast corner of Iowa. Tucked into a valley between
river bluffs, Lansing was a remote outpost on the main channel of
the Mississippi River.

Communication with the outside world was sporadic. Mail
arrived every week or two, sent up from Galena, Illinois, the
packet thrown to shore from the passing boat, weighted with
a stone picked up at the last landing.[1] Riverboats passed by
just a few times a month, stopping only for wood or to land
the occasional passenger. But Lansing's landing was handy for
steamboats in all seasons of navigation, and it would eventually
become a key supply point for the region.

In 1851, things were just starting to happen for this little settlement. It was platted that year by John Haney Sr., his son, James, and Horace H. Houghton, a newspaper editor from Galena. The State of Iowa had been officially admitted to the Union five years earlier and was encouraging pioneers. Public land in Allamakee, the county in the very northeast corner, had become available for purchase the previous October. European settlers, forced to emigrate by the potato famine in Ireland and political upheaval in Germany, were moving into the area by the wagonload. At the same time, the few remaining members of the Winnebago Tribe were leaving.

The Winnebago had been moved into northeast Iowa twenty years earlier, when the United States government designated a 40-mile wide strip of land the Neutral Zone. Designed as a buffer between two warring tribes, the Sioux and Sac & Fox, the Neutral Zone had been dismantled just a few years earlier, in 1948. All remaining tribe members were being removed so the land could be opened up for settlers.

This would be the decade that transformed the Lansing area, and all of Allamakee County, from a frontier wilderness to a thriving Euro-American settlement. Lansing's first frame building was erected that year, at the corner of Main and Front, a mercantile for the first storekeeper, F.D. Cowles. Cowles' son, Frank, would be the first boy born in the community. Elisha Hale built a factory along the river, where he planned to manufacture farm machinery; his daughter, Alberta, the first girl born. The first frame hotel, the Lansing House, was built on Front Street that fall. Lansing also had a sawmill, a gristmill, a saloon, and a handful of houses.

The population was small, recorded at 80 in 1850.[2] It would grow five-fold to 440 by 1854. Lansing wouldn't be incorporated as a town until 1867, another 16 years. The first train wouldn't appear for 20 years, until 1872. By then the population would have grown to 2,280 residents.

It was late spring when the steamboat that carried Hatty approached Lansing. Decades later, H.H. Houghton, recalled the events of the day:

> *"It was said by one of the boys that if ladies were not so awkward in climbing, they would propose a match. Miss Hosmer, then a gay, romping, athletic schoolgirl, proffered a wager that she could reach the summit more quickly than any of them, whereupon the captain tied up the boat and they went on shore. The race was made, and Miss Hosmer was the victor."[3]*

To celebrate her win, a couple of Lansing's prominent settlers agreed to name the bluff "Mount Hosmer."

Martha L. Hemenway, the daughter of John Haney Sr., was the last living witness to the events that day. She told a slightly different story when interviewed by author Albert S. Tousley when she was eighty-five years old.

> *"I remember it well," Mrs. Hemenway recalled. "It was June 1851, when Miss Hosmer made her memorable ascent of the now famous bluff. She was taking a trip up the river on*

Captain Orrin Smith's steamboat, the Senator. I was ten and one-half years old and much interested. The crew was taking on wood..... Miss Hosmer came out onto the bow of the boat and was talking to the captain about the beautiful scenery. She asked Captain Smith how long they were going to stay.

"As long as you wish," he replied gallantly.

"Will I have time to climb that bluff?

"We will give you time.

"Captain Smith called a clerk to accompany her. She soon outdistanced him, and stood alone on the brow of the hill, waving her handkerchief to the stewardess, who was on the guard of the boat, ringing the breakfast bell. Coming down, she met her escort half way up. She ran gleefully past him, returning the victor in the race.

"Before he went back to the boat, the clerk asked her to wait while he went to our house. There he interviewed the proprietors. Fortunately, both were present. He asked whether the bluff had a name, and was told 'not as yet.' Then he requested that the bluff be named Mount Hosmer, in honor of the lady who had just made the record ascent. Miss Hosmer seemed pleased, but she probably did not realize that the old bluff would stand a living memorial to her, long after she had gone to her last rest. This was quite an event and a very happy experience in my rather uneventful life.

I still have a vivid recollection of the bright young girl who chatted so pleasantly with me about the wild strawberries *and flowers growing near."* [4]

Harriet was amused to learn many years later that the name still stood. An obscure beginning to a lifetime of accomplishments and notoriety, she would go on to become one of the most celebrated women of her era. Symbolic of her future path, Hatty's winning run up the hill demonstrated a willingness to forge a trail into uncharted territory. She had the strength and courage to lead the way into places others dared not go. Even in her youth, she was a "symbol of independence and a woman's right to determine her own destiny."[5]

---

[1] Ellery Hancock, *Past and Present of Allamakee County, Volume 1, Illustrated*, (Chicago: S.J. Clarke Publishing Company, 1913), 416.

[2] Lansing Iowa on the Mississippi 1867-1967, (Centennial booklet, 1967), 59.

[3] Carr, HH L&M, 12.

[4] Albert S. Tousley, *Where the River Goes*, (Iowa City, Iowa: The Tepee Press, 1928), 94.

[5] Sherwood, 8.

"The Hosmers are the most crooked sticks that God or the Devil ever concocted."

6

⁂

Taking Her Place
as an Artist

The months spent in St. Louis and traveling on the Mississippi were a training exercise for the greater adventure that lay ahead for Hatty. She proved that she could be "independent of chaperone and companion," an extraordinary departure at the time from the "prescribed rules for young women of good background."[1]

Harriet Hosmer returned to Watertown ready to work. With her father's help, she transformed a small structure in the backyard into an art studio. She also took over a room on the first floor of her father's house, which she filled with objects she collected in her romps through the woods. A visitor noted, "She had ducks, fowls of every description in our climate, curious twigs and branches, grasses, ferns, in fact everything a resolute girl of her peculiar taste and with such a venturesome spirit might collect."[2] There were more than five hundred types of butterflies mounted between panes of the front window, reptiles in bottles of alcohol, turtle shells, and deer antlers. New additions to her collection were nuggets and ore from the Iowa lead mine, and a peace pipe brought home from her river travels. A live snake named Eve was soon joined by a pet monkey, which Hatty described in a letter to Cornelia Crow as "the most mischievous, ludicrous, funny thing you ever knew."[3]

Harriet's first sculpting project was a medallion, made as a gift for Dr. McDowell, the professor at the Missouri Medical College who supported her studies of anatomy. She then completed a bust of Napoleon for her father before beginning a bust of the mythological maiden of the Eastern Star, Hesper, inspired by the imagery in Tennyson's recently published, *In Memoriam*, a poem of deep loss, divine questioning, and transformation. Hatty "lost her wits over it,"[4] memorizing many of the verses.

In mythology, Hesperus, the son of the dawn goddess, Eos, was the first to climb Mount Atlas to watch the stars. Swept away by a storm, he disappeared without a trace, said to have transformed into the lovely evening star, Venus, which brings the peace of night.

Harriet's finished sculpture, *Hesper, the Evening Star* (1852), became an object of local acclaim and admiration. Many were astonished that the sculptor was a petite woman, whose delicate hands had executed the creation from clay model to marble entirely alone, a feat of physical strength and endurance. Harriet, "carefully but surely directing the chisel with the ponderous mallet, worked eight to ten hours a day in her determined effort to finish the work."[5] This work ethic would become a hallmark of her professional life.

Harriet's work caught the attention of Lydia Maria Child, who had lived next to the Hosmers in her youth and whose husband David was an old friend of Hiram Hosmer's. Child was one of the most famous and respected women authors of the day, active in nearly every area of social reform, including abolition, women's rights, religious freedom, prison reform, and the fight against capital punishment. Her pamphlet, "*An Appeal in Favor of That Class of Americans Called Africans (1833)*," was the first antislavery literature published in America.[6]

Mrs. Child soon became one of Harriet's most powerful allies, using her connections and influence to publicize Harriet's work by writing a rave review of *Hesper* for the *New York Tribune*. She wrote poetically:

"This beautiful production has the face of a lovely maiden gently falling asleep to the sound of distant music. Her hair is gracefully intertwined with capsules of the poppy. A polished star gleams on her forehead, and under her breast lies the crescent moon. The hush of evening breathes from the serene countenance and the heavily-drooping eyelids … the swell of cheek and breast is like pure, young, healthy flesh, and the

muscles of the beautiful mouth are so delicately cut, that it
seems a thing that breathes."[7]

The piece, published anonymously, was titled "*A New Star in the Arts*," and it launched Harriet as a serious artist.

During this time, Harriet met Charlotte Cushman, the most celebrated actress of the era and a native of Boston. Harriet was taken backstage by a friend to meet the greatly admired actress when Cushman was in her native city for a professional engagement. They quickly became friends. When Charlotte learned that Hatty was developing her skills as a sculptor, she immediately took an interest in the young artist. Using her wealth and prestige, Cushman had long taken an active role in encouraging women in the arts. Hatty's future was surely a subject of conversation.

It was inevitable that Harriet would be drawn to Italy. Admired around the world for its artistic environment, Rome was a haven for poets, scholars, travelers, and artists. It was the destination of choice for American sculptors, with access to marble, workmen, living models, and the best training.

When Charlotte Cushman made plans to go to Rome that fall to rest and contemplate retirement, she offered to include Hatty in her household. It was a wonderful opportunity, but not an easy decision for the Hosmers. Revolutionary activity in Italy was pushing the country toward unification, and there had been several uprisings and battles in recent years. The status of the papacy in question, Pope Pius IX had been forced into exile. With efforts underway to establish a Roman republic, the situation was unsettled and unpredictable.

Harriet expressed her fears in a letter to Cornelia Carr in January 1852: "The only thought that troubles me is, that I fear before another twelve months have passed, Italy, if not the whole of Europe, will be plunged in war."[8]

Despite her concerns, Harriet was determined to go. Dr. Hosmer gave his consent, and the packing and planning got underway. Hardly able to contain her anticipation, Harriet wrote, "I feel that I am on the eve of a new life—that the earth will look larger, the sky brighter, the world in general more grand."[9]

---

[1] Sherwood, 33.

[2] Culkin, 21.

[3] Sherwood, 34.

[4] Ibid, 45.

[5] Culkin, 24.

[6] Sherwood, 36.

[7] Carr, HH L&M, 16.

[8] Ibid.

[9] Ibid, 18.

"The only impediments to progress are those created by a mind unwilling to confront its own vast potential."

7

✳

JOINING THE MASTERS IN ROME

In November 1852, at age 22, Harriet Hosmer, arrived in Rome. With two daguerreotypes of *Hesper, the Evening Star,* and her certificate of proficiency in anatomy, the young artist was accepted for study under the guidance of one of the greatest sculptors in Italy at the time, the English neoclassicist John Gibson. Gibson was at the peak of his career and had just completed a full-length statue of Queen Victoria, the highest accolade imaginable for a British sculptor.[1]

Harriet settled into a workroom in Gibson's studio where the famous Italian sculptor Antonio Canova once worked. To reach it, visitors passed through a gallery filled with Gibson's work, crossed a garden bright with flowers and ferns, and ascended steps into a small workroom where sunlight streamed in through an arched window."[2] Here she would work for the next seven years.

To test her skill, Gibson put Harriet to work copying classical statues in sizes other than their original form. She worked diligently and took in everything that Gibson had to teach her. When he was satisfied with the "correctness of her eye,"[3] she began working on her own concepts, infusing them with her own creative touch.

A close bond quickly grew between Gibson and Hosmer. While the foundation of their relationship was always master and student, an element of playfulness was evident in their interactions. He teased her about her "diminutive size," and his devotion to her was clear in personal notes he signed "Your slave."[4] He became a kind friend and wise master. "I am convinced Heaven smiled most benignantly upon me when it sent me to him," Harriet said.[5]

British actress Fanny Kemble, who knew Hatty well from her years at Mrs. Sedgwick's, spoke of Harriet's potential in a letter to Wayman Crow: "I think she will distinguish herself greatly, for she is not only gifted with an unusual artistic capacity, but she has energy, perseverance, and industry; attributes often wanting where genius exists, and extremely seldom possessed or exercised in any effectual manner by women."[6]

Frances Power Cobbe, an Irish activist and writer, fondly wrote of her impression when Harriet first arrived in Rome. "She was in those days the most bewitching sprite that the world ever saw…with an inexhaustible flow of wit, drollery, and genial joyous humor. Never have I laughed so helplessly as at the infinite fun of that bright Yankee girl."[7]

Harriet joined a large international circle of artists and
writers in Rome, their names reading like a Who's Who list
of literary giants of the time. Among them were English artist
Frederic Leighton; writers Nathaniel Hawthorne, William
Thackeray, Hans Christian Andersen, Henry Wadsworth
Longfellow, Harriet Beecher Stowe, and Henry James; and poets
Robert and Elizabeth Barrett Browning.

From the time they met in the winter of 1853 until Elizabeth's
death in June, 1861, Harriet and the Brownings were close friends.
The two women had much in common, both lost their mother at
an early age, had active outdoor childhoods, and were precocious
learners. Both Robert and Elizabeth wrote often to "Hattie," and
with their young son, Penini, visited her in Rome.

Elizabeth Barrett Browning wrote of the young American
sculptress, "who is a great pet of mine and Robert's, and who
emancipates the eccentric life of a perfectly 'emancipated female'
from all shadow of blame by the purity of hers. She lives here all
alone (at twenty-two); dines and breakfasts at the cafes precisely
as a young man would; works from six o'clock in the morning
till night, as a great artist must, and this with an absence of
pretension and simplicity of manners which accord rather with
the childish dimples in her rosy cheeks than with her broad
forehead and high aims."[8]

Other expatriate American sculptors, including Edmonia
Lewis, Emma Stebbins, Mary Lloyd, and Vinnie Ream, joined
Harriet in Rome over the years, encouraged by her success. Henry

James disparagingly referred to them as "that strange Sisterhood of American 'lady sculptors' who settled upon the seven hills in a white marmorean flock." James, like many conservatives of his day, was disturbed by their unladylike independence and disregard of traditional social rules. While these sculptors received considerable attention, and numerous commissions, they were laughed at by many.[9] Despite his criticism, Henry James acknowledged that Harriet was "above all a character, strong, fresh, and interesting."[10]

The task of sculpting was intensely physical and demanding, the artist often working from a high platform in an atmosphere clammy with the moisture needed for the clay. Harriet used a mallet that weighed four pounds, swinging it for over eight hours a day. It was work that challenged assumptions about female strength and ability.

Not only did many believe women were incapable of meeting the physically demanding nature of the work, they saw women as inherently lacking in creativity and originality. A fellow sculptor of the time, William Story, revealed this idea clearly when he commented on the young artist's work: "It is one thing to copy and another to create. She may or may not have inventive powers as an artist. If she have, will she not be the first woman who ever had?"[11]

Story's notion was prevalent, a concept so universally accepted at the time that it was seen as truth and rarely questioned or disputed. But in testimony to her character,

Harriet eventually forged a lasting bond of friendship with Story and his family.

Harriet took to wearing a man-tailored shirt, a cravat, a skirt or large bloomer-like pants, and a purple smock. She wore her curly hair short, topped by a velvet sculptor's hat. Creating the impression of a young boy, she was allowed the freedom to ride and walk the streets of Rome unescorted and to eat alone in the cafes near her studio. Her midnight horse rides were the talk of the city, as riding—or even walking—alone in Rome was an uncommon thing for a woman to do.

The majority of sales for American artists in Rome came from fellow countrymen traveling through Europe. Guidebooks offered the artists addresses and descriptions of their latest work. It was common for well-to-do Americans to visit a sculptor's studio to have their portrait done and to look over the plaster models, often choosing one or more for reproduction in marble.

Over the years, a steady stream of tourists climbed to Harriet's second-story studio to catch a glimpse of the unusual artist at work. Mark Twain was one. Nathaniel Hawthorne another. Hawthorne visited her studio in Rome in 1858, when Harriet was 28, and later gave a vivid description: "We found Miss Hosmer is a little up-stairs room. She is a small, brisk, wide-awake figure, of queer and funny aspect… she seems so frank, simple, straightforward, and downright."[12]

Hawthorne continued, "She had on petticoats, I think; but I did not look so low, my attention being chiefly drawn to a sort of man's sack of purple or plum-colored broadcloth, into the side-pockets of which her hands were thrust as she came forward to greet us…her face was bright and funny, and as small of feature as a child's. It looked, in one aspect, youthful and yet there was something worn in it, too, as if it had faced a good deal of wind and weather, either morally or physically."[13]

Hawthorne wrote in defense of her unusual attire, "she seemed to be her actual self, and nothing affected or made-up; so that, for my part, I give her full leave to wear what may suit her best, and to behave as her inner woman prompts."[14]

Hawthorne and Harriet quickly became friends and he and his family would return to visit her often.

Harriet took great pride in her work. The pieces she created were an extension of her, a part of her soul out-pictured in sculpture. She often referred to them as her children, her marble sons and daughters. Yet, as important as it was to her to be a great artist, it was even more important to her to be a good person. This she made clear in a message written in 1855 to her two-month-old godchild and namesake Harriet Hosmer Carr, the daughter of Cornelia and Lucien Carr:

"Still better than being a great artist it will be, to be great as a human being. This is to have your heart filled with beautiful and kindly thoughts for all around you, as well as to have your brain filled with beautiful images, though you know you can never have the latter without the former, for your marble children would be only the sculptured shadows of your

soul, and if your soul is not pure and great, how can you expect your children to be so?"[15]

Sadly, Harriet would feel the heartbreak of another tragic loss, when Harriet Hosmer Carr died of kidney failure in 1880, at the age of 25.[16]

---

[1] Sherwood, 54.

[2] Carr, HH L&M, 22.

[3] Sherwood, 62.

[4] Ibid, 64

[5] Ibid, 23.

[6] Carr, HH L&M, 28.

[7] Ibid.

[8] Michele Martinez, *Sister Arts and Artists: Elizabeth Barrett Browning's Aurora Leigh and the Life of Harriet Hosmer,* (Court of the University of St. Andrews, 2003) 6.

[9] Karen Petersen & J.J. Wilson, Women Artists: Recognition & Reappraisal From the Early Middle Ages to the Twentieth Century, (Harper Colophon Books, 1976), 79.

[10] Culkin, 3.

[11] Sherwood, 22.

[12] Ibid, 3.

[13] Ibid, 4.

[14] Thorp, p. 86 or Sherwood p.4

[15] Carr, HH L&M, 55.

[16] Sherwood, 322.

"Live well, do well, and all will be well."

8

✳

THE PROCESS
OF SCULPTURE

Sculpting in marble was arduous, and Harriet impressed many people with her endurance, determination, and skill when she created *Hester, the Evening Star* while in Watertown. In moving to Rome, she knew that she would no longer have to do all of the labor-intensive work on her own.

A well-staffed studio like Gibson's had a number of skilled artisans, apprentices, and marble cutters involved in the process of bringing an artist's concept to life. This method became widely accepted in the nineteenth century when sculptors were unable to personally carve all of the pieces that were ordered.

The first step in the process was the idea, with the artist fully envisioning the piece in their mind. This step is where Harriet's contemporaries understood the creative genius to lie. Artists would then create a clay model, usually much smaller than the finished product would be. This would be a detailed and exacting process, often requiring several versions to perfect the design. When the artist was satisfied with the model, the studio workers whose specialty it was built a skeleton strong enough to support the weight of a full-size clay model.

Harriet once described the process: "It took a blacksmith heating irons and bending them to the angles needed for the structure. Wood and wire were added, their shape and size corresponding to the size and shape of the projected figure. They had to be crisscrossed, laced, and intertwined."[1]

This was all done to support the heavy mass of clay. Workmen pressed great blobs of it upon the skeleton then used strong hands and a wooden mallet to transform the shapeless mass into some semblance of the intended form.

The sculptor then returned to the piece for the greater part of the task, infusing into the clay the refinement and beauty of their style, attending to every detail, bringing the creation to life. This fine-tuning often took many weeks or months and was also intensely physical and demanding.

When the clay model was finished, as perfect as possible in the eye of the artist, the work passed again from the sculptor's hands. It was first enveloped in plaster to create a full-size pattern for replication and then passed on to the marble workers. These were highly skilled artisans who would transfer the pattern mechanically, duplicating the sculptor's dimensions or making them larger or smaller as needed. After the first heavy blocking out of the marble with a chisel, increasingly more intricate tools were used to bring out the details and add the finishing touches. The role of the sculptor at this point, was merely to direct and correct the work as it proceeded.

The final step was to polish the marble, bringing forth the beauty of its pure white color and rich, smooth surface.

This method was essential to the financial success of the sculptors in Rome. It freed them to produce more work, plus gave them time to make contacts and promote themselves. It also allowed for multiple replicas of a piece.

---

[1] Sherwood, 61.

"Every woman should have the opportunity of cultivating her talents to the fullest extent, for they were not given her for nothing."

9

✳

HARRIET'S MAJOR WORKS

Like her mentor Gibson, Harriet worked in the neoclassical style popular in her day, often depicting mythological figures and themes. "There is something in the purity of the marble, in the perfect calmness…of a beautiful statue," she said.[1] Harriet was prolific in Rome, and her sculptures were considered extraordinary. Her work offered a passion and a depth of expression that was markedly unlike that of her contemporaries.

In her work, "Harriet strove for synthesis of beautiful forms, physical truths, and pathos."[2] She explored themes of female victimization, as well as feminine power, revealing her compassion and sensitivity to the plight of women throughout history. She also created several works recognizing the courage of ordinary people facing extraordinary challenges.

DAPHNE

The bust *Daphne* (1853) was Harriet's first original work in Rome. The poet Ovid in *Metamorphoses* told the story of the mythological maiden Daphne, who vowed perpetual virginity, preferring to run free in the forest rather than accept the bonds of love or marriage. Renouncing the love of the god Apollo, she was saved from his relentless pursuit by being turned into a laurel tree.

The finished *Daphne* was simple and graceful. The face was classically styled, the eyes unworked. The shoulders and breasts were bare, exhibiting a skill described by Gibson as "never surpassed and seldom equaled."[3]

Harriet made two copies, one to be displayed in Gibson's studio, and the other was sent to Cornelia Crow.

THE CLASPED HANDS

Hosmer memorialized one of her great friendships in her next piece, *The Clasped Hands of Robert Browning and Elizabeth Barrett Browning*. In admiration of their equitable relationship, Harriet made a mold of the couple's joined right hands, Robert's palm closed protectively around his wife's small hand. Harriet clearly admired the Browning's equitable marriage. She also believed that their hands had given the world some of its finest poetry.[4]

This was Harriet's first work in bronze. There are ten known casts of this work, and it is probable that more were created.

MEDUSA

Medusa (1854), a companion piece to *Daphne*, was Harriet's first commissioned sculpture.

In Greek mythology, Medusa was the only mortal and the most beautiful of the three Gorgon sisters. She had an affair with Poseidon, which caused Athena to retaliate, transforming Medusa into a repulsive being with snakes for hair and a gaze that turned men into stone.

Harriet's portrayal was not the standard image of dread, but one of a beautiful woman, made horrific against her will. It was described as "faultless in form, while intense in its expression of grief and agony at the transformation, although it leaves her beautiful still."[5]

Medusa was shipped to Boston, where it was put on exhibition and purchased by merchant and philanthropist Samuel Appleton. The city of Appleton, Wisconsin, was eventually named in his honor.

OENONE

Harriet created her first full-length, full-sized figure, *Oenone* (1855), inspired by a poem by Alfred Lord Tennyson. Oenone was the woman whom Paris loved but abandoned to pursue Helen of Troy. In a rare depiction of her mourning, Harriet captured Oenone's betrayal and rejection, her head bowed in utter dejection, her body heavy with sadness.

The *London Art Journal* described the work: "This statue

portrays Oenone in deep and speechless grief at the death of Paris. The face is of classic beauty, the drapery strikingly natural, and the position of the body bending over a shepherd's crook on one hand, while the other hangs listlessly by her side, is expressive in the highest degree of the grief which the artist has sought to embody."[6]

This piece was sent to her St. Louis patron, Wayman Crow.

PUCK

During this same period, Harriet completed the playful and imaginative, *Puck*, a small marble cherub seated on a toadstool, which became one of her most popular works.

In a letter to Wayman Crow in February 1857, Harriet described her creation from Shakespeare's *A Midsummer Night's Dream* as "a laugh in marble." She wrote: "This little forest elf is the very personification of boyish self-will and mischief. With his right hand he grasps a beetle, and seems about to throw it; with his left he presses unconsciously a lizard. In all the lines of the face, in all the action of the body, gleams forth the mischievous self-will of a being scarcely aware of the pain he causes, while rollicking in the consciousness of his tiny might."[7]

Harriet created *Puck* out of financial necessity when her father's financial status took a downward turn and he could no longer support her in Rome. It was the sculpture that would ultimately bring her the most money and fame of all her works. It became an instant success with the aristocracy. *Puck* was purchased by the Prince of Wales in 1859, at the time still a youth in his teens. The eldest son of Queen Victoria, he would later be crowned King Edward VII.

Over the years, 30 reproductions of the cast of *Puck* were created, selling for $500 to $1,000 each, finding their way to public galleries and private art collections in both Europe and America. Twelve known versions remain today.

WILL-O'-THE-WISP

A companion for *Puck*, was *Will-o'-the-Wisp* (1856). Also inspired by Shakespeare's *A Midsummer Night's Dream*, Will is a marshland fairy who could adopt a phosphorescent glow and had a habit of scaring lost travelers.

The sculpture was reworked in two additional variations (1858, 1864). None of the three versions was able to duplicate the fame or financial success of Puck.

BEATRICE CENCI

Harriet's next project was a more challenging sculpture and her first full-size work of a historical figure. *Beatrice Cenci* (1856) was commissioned by the St. Louis Mercantile Library and through special invitation, displayed at the Royal Academy in London.

The story of Beatrice Cenci was well-known and written of in Rome while Harriet lived there. Beatrice's father, the Roman count Francesco Cenci, was a corrupt 16th-century aristocrat notorious for his immoral conduct. It was said that he sexually assaulted his 16-year-old daughter, Beatrice, and with her stepmother and brothers, she plotted to kill him to escape the abuse. Legend tells that a corrupt Pope subsequently brought her and her family members to trial and she was eventually beheaded.

Harriet's sculpture was a heartrending image of a young woman lying down in a childlike pose, her limp hand clutching a rosary, ready to find salvation in an afterlife. *The New York Times* raved about the creation, "The conception of the statue is masterly… it is exceedingly bold and original without being overstrained and striking without being affected."[8]

Lydia Marie Child again praised Harriet's work: "Especially do I rejoice that such a poetical conception of the subject came from a woman's soul, and that such finished workmanship was done by a woman's hand."[9]

TOMB OF JUDITH FALCONNET

In 1857, Harriet was commissioned to carve the tomb sculpture for 16-year-old Judith de Palezieux Falconnet for the Church of Sant'Andrea della Fratte. With this commission Harriet became the first American to create a tomb for a Catholic church in Rome.

The life-sized sculpture shows the girl in solemn dignity, lying on a couch with her feet crossed, as if taking a nap. She holds a rosary in one hand, while the other has fallen by her side. The peaceful, sleeping face was made in Falconnet's likeness, created by the sculptor working from a death mask.

A letter written to the young girl's mother commended Harriet's work, "It has exceeded every expectation I had formed of it. The unaffected simplicity and tender feeling displayed in the treatment are all that could be desired for such a subject and cannot fail to touch the most casual observer … I feel sure that you could not have raised a monument to your lamented daughter's memory in any way more worthy of her."[10]

Zenobia in Chains

Harriet's work environment changed in late 1858, when she moved into her own studio at 5 Via Margutta, "a lofty room, with a sky-light window … and a small orange tree in a pot."[11] She had gotten a commission too big to complete in her small space in Gibson's studio.

Zenobia in Chains was created in 1859, and mentioned by Nathaniel Hawthorne in the preface of his work, *The Marble Faun*. Standing over seven feet tall, the statue depicted the third-century Queen of Palmyra (now Syria), who ruled the country after her husband's death. The queen was captured by the Romans in 270 A.D. and put on display to be ridiculed in her jewels and finery. Harriet's image portrayed the queen's serene resolve, emphasizing her strength, as well as her beauty.

Exhibited at the renowned Crystal Palace in London in 1862, the statue was so successful that there was speculation it had been created by Harriet's mentor, John Gibson, a charge he flatly

Harriet Hosmer arrived in Lansing on the *Senator*, with Captain Orrin Smith at the helm.

Harriet with *Daphne*, her first original sculpture in Rome.

The Clasped Hands of Robert Browning and Elizabeth Barrett Browning was a tribute to Harriet's dear friends.

Typically portrayed as a hideous woman with snakes for hair, Harriet presented a different perspective of the beautiful *Medusa*.

Harriet's first full-length, full-sized sculpture, *Oenone* was inspired by the poetry of Alfred Lord Tennyson.

The mischievous *Puck* was Harriet's most popular piece.

The marshland fairy *Will-o'-the-Wisp* was reworked in three variations.

Beatrice Cenci captured the tragic story of a Roman girl's abuse at the hands of her father.

The imposing *Zenobia in Chains*, standing over seven feet tall, was seen by record-breaking crowds in New York during the summer of 1864.

This photograph of Harriet working on the statue of *Thomas Hart Benton* offers a striking perspective of the dimension of her work.

The Prince of Wales purchased the *Sleeping Faun* for his private collection.

Real photo postcard views of the fountain *The Mermaid's Cradle* were common at the turn of the century.

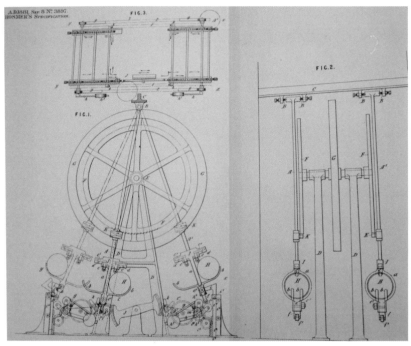

Harriet spent years creating plans for a perpetual motion machine.

Visitors to the lookout near the top of Mount Hosmer enjoy a breathtaking view of the Upper Mississippi River Valley, with the historic Blackhawk Bridge in the foreground.

The bluffs roll along the river northward in a 50-mile panoramic view of Iowa, Wisconsin, and Minnesota.

H.H. Houghton, one of Lansing's earliest settlers and most likely one of the men who agreed to the name, wrote in 1888 about Harriet's visit and the events of that day. His home, built in 1863, sits on the side of Mount Hosmer.

A veterans memorial, established on the land atop Mount Hosmer in 1922, was rededicated in 2001. The city park also includes hiking trails, lookout points, and picnic and play areas.

denied. The sculpture was taken to New York in the summer of 1864, and later displayed at the Jenks Art Gallery in Boston, where it was seen by record-breaking crowds.

An anonymous author in the *Saturday Evening Gazette* wrote, "Will not–shall not–every American look with pride–an honest, noble pride–on this marble effigy of Zenobia, because it is the ideal, the production, of an American, and that American a woman."[12]

The full-size *Zenobia in Chains*, lost for decades, was found in an outdoor garden and sold at a Sotheby's auction in 2008 to the Huntington Library in San Marino, California. Another version of this statue was purchased for the luxurious home of Chicago financier Potter Palmer.

THOMAS HART BENTON

In 1860, Harriet received a commission from the city of St. Louis for a statue of Thomas Hart Benton, a Missouri senator for thirty years. Competition for the coveted commission was fierce and winning it was a huge professional victory for the artist.

Cast in bronze, the greater than life-sized monument stands about 15 feet high in Lafayette Park, St. Louis, where it was dedicated in 1868, becoming the first public monument in the state of Missouri. The statue depicts Benton draped in a cloak similar to one he frequently wore. Using the cloak precluded the need for Harriet to model the upper part of Benton's trousered legs, which would have been considered unfeminine in the nineteenth century.[13]

CHALLENGES OF THE EARLY 1860's

The Hart Benton commission was a lone bright spot as the decade of the 1860s settled in. This would prove to be a difficult time for Harriet. The Civil War broke out in April 1861, casting a pall over the expatriate population in Rome. Just a few months later, Elizabeth Barrett Browning unexpectedly died. Harriet wrote to Cornelia of her relationship with Browning: "To have seen her and to have been admitted to her friendship, I must always consider as one of the happiest circumstances of my life." Harriet thought Elizabeth's character reflected the highest degree of beauty that human nature could attain.[14]

Within a year, on April 15, 1862, Harriet's father Hiram died. Harriet said little about it, for "of her sorrows she could not speak."[15]

In the latter part of 1864, Harriet's work came under fire. There had been veiled comments for years that she did not do her own work, but the rumors had not found a wide audience or impacted her career. Now the circumstances were different. Fatherless and working in her own studio, Harriet was no longer under male control and direction. She had found great success with *Zenobia in Chains*, which struck a chord with those who believed a woman incapable of such precise and labor-intensive work.

As a female artist receiving frequent commissions and a significant amount of high-profile attention, Hosmer knew that she was unpopular with her male counterparts. She was no longer a novelty or easy to dismiss. Lesser-known male artists viewed the young woman's growing success as the reason for their failure, believing she took commissions that should have been theirs. Snide remarks and innuendos were unceasing and insidious, even suggesting that she had an inappropriate relationship with Gibson.

The challenge to her integrity reached public attention when an obituary published for sculptor Alfred Gatley appeared in the English publication, *The Queen*. The obituary, written anonymously, said that Gatley's work had not gotten the attention it deserved, overlooked "beside the more meretricious charms" of Zenobia, "said to be by Miss Hosmer but really executed by an Italian workman in Rome."[16] When the widely read and influential *Art Journal* quoted the remarks, Harriet faced a serious challenge to her reputation.

In a time when women rarely raised their voices against injustice, Harriet spoke up. She quickly responded to the accusation by filing a libel suit against those who made the claims and, in her defense, wrote a step-by-step article for the magazine, *The Atlantic Monthly*. Her article, titled "The Process of Sculpture," gave an in-depth and detailed description of the sculptural process used throughout Italy, by sculptors of *both* genders. She confronted the jealousy of her fellow male artists in a poem published in the *New York Evening Post*, titled "The Doleful Ditty of The Roman Caffe Greco," using satire to point out their chauvinism. One particularly barbed section read:

"Suppose you try another plan,
More worthy art and you;
Suppose you give them for their works
The credit which is due.

"An honest and a kindly word,
If spoken now and then,
Would prove what seems a doubtful point
You could, at least, be men."

Harriet claimed damages of one thousand pounds but withdrew her suit when apologies were printed in the publications involved.

Sleeping Faun / Waking Faun

In 1865 Harriet created the fanciful *Sleeping Faun*, which received great acclaim at the Dublin International Exposition. A Dublin newspaper reported: "It is universally admired, and is more frequently the subject of conversation than any other statue in the exhibition."[17] Sir Benjamin Guinness purchased the piece for $5,000 on the opening day of the Exposition for the City of Dublin,[18] an equivalent of over $70,000 today. In the 1870s, the Prince of Wales purchased a copy to add to his private collection.[19]

The faun in Roman mythology (like the satyr in Greek mythology) was a woodland spirit that was half human and half goat. In Harriet's sculpture, the faun is sleeping peacefully, resting against a tree stump. The details of her work added an element of humor and neutralized the sexuality of the character, which had she not done so, would have crossed the limits of decorum acceptable at that time.

A companion sculpture, *Waking Faun*, a mirror opposite of the *Sleeping Faun*, was designed in 1866-67, but it is doubtful that it was ever put into marble. In Harriet's words, "… it fell far too short of the other and I never could make it go–it was no good–it was in no manner, style, modeling, sentiment nor anything else, the worthy companion of the other."[20]

WAYMAN CROW

In 1868, Harriet surprised Wayman Crow with a bust she made of him. It was given as a gift to Washington University School of Medicine, the school that evolved from the program in which she studied anatomy so many years before. "The bust, of white marble, rests upon a polished pedestal of a darker shade…the face wears a calm and noble expression, a look full of meaning, an indescribable something which shows the work to be no less the language of the artist's heart, than a faithful likeness of her friend."[21] Inscribed on its base are the words, "Tribute of Gratitude," Harriet's way of expressing her appreciation for their friendship and for the professional support he had given her through her career.

QUEEN OF NAPLES

Also in 1868, Harriet created her only other full-length figure of a contemporary figure, depicting the tragic warrior queen Maria Sophia, the beautiful ex-queen of Naples.

The queen and her husband, King Francis II, had fought against the occupation of Naples, taking the last stand against the forces of United Italy. Maria Sophia had become a heroine to European royal women, as she fought bravely beside her husband through that final battle. Forced to surrender, the royal couple accepted Pope Pius IX's offer of asylum in Rome.

Harriet and the ex-queen became friends during her exile. Maria Sophia visited the artist's studio frequently, posing for the statue so that the likeness would be perfect. The life-size marble statue was said to have captured the queen's most heroic moments on the battlegrounds of Gaeta, a long billowing military cape enveloping her as she stood strong, her hair braided and woven like a crown on her head, the look on her face expressing both disdain and resolution.

Many thought this work was Hosmer's masterpiece, but its location is unknown. It was mentioned in newpaper accounts, art magazines, and personal correspondence, but no visual documentation of the statue survives.

Harriet continued to visit the disposed king and queen when they moved to Germany in 1870. At some point she made a sculpture of a staghound for Maria Sophia's sister Elisabeth, the empress of Austria.

LINCOLN MEMORIAL/THE AFRICAN SIBYL

From 1888 to 1896, Harriet worked on a fourth and final attempt to win a Lincoln Memorial commission. Wealthy Chicago financier, John Crerar, left a $100,000 bequest for a statue to be made in honor of the assassinated president. *African Sibyl*, which Harriet had begun as an independent work, became one part of the more elaborate three-figure design proposed for the Crerar competition.

Harriet's proposal portrayed an ancient female prophet foretelling the future of her race to an African male child seated at her feet. She is looking hopefully at Lincoln, holding a scroll that quotes him, "If slavery is not wrong nothing is wrong."

It was a long complicated competition, drawn out over six years due to a lawsuit against the estate by Crerar's distant relatives. Harriet exchanged numerous letters with the memorial committee over these years, explaining different problems she had creating, shipping, and delivering the model. It is unclear if the committee ever saw her design.

Alfred Lord Tennyson wrote of her design, saying: "It is the most poetic rendering in art of a great historical truth I have ever seen."[22]

THE MERMAID'S CRADLE

Harriet Hosmer also created several fountains for great estates in England, including a pair in marble commissioned by Lady Louisa Ashburton for her country house in Hampshire. Known to still be there in 1903, today their whereabouts are unknown. However, one of them, *The Mermaid's Cradle*, was replicated in bronze in 1893 and adorns Fountain Square in Flint Park, Larchmont, New York. It was often featured on postcards of Larchmont at the turn of the century.

The design is of a mermaid playing a pipe, her muscular torso nude from the waist up. Waves of water crash around her hips as she sits on the rocky coast. Her long, scaled tail curls around a sleeping baby mermaid.

Although the patina has been damaged by weather and pollution, the form is intact and the fountain appears to work. It is Harriet's only remaining complete fountain.

Queen Isabella

Harriet's final historical sculpture was the figure of *Queen Isabella of Spain*, created for the Columbian Exposition in Chicago in 1893. The Daughters of Isabella, a Chicago-based suffragist organization, commissioned the piece, recognizing that Harriet's art "helped to lift the women of the century to a higher level."[23]

Harriet thought Isabella to be a perfect subject for the world exposition celebrating the anniversary of Columbus discovering America. She portrayed her as a co-discoverer of the New World, but the work provoked strong controversy. Some saw Isabella as a religious bigot and a cruel leader who funded the Inquisition; others saw her as a compassionate visionary.

The statue of Queen Isabella was later sent to San Francisco, with a plan to install it permanently in Golden Gate Park. Art historians speculate that it was destroyed in the earthquake and fire of 1906.

ADDITIONAL SCULPTURES

One of the most notable of Harriet's works that was designed but never materialized was titled *Golden Gates*. Harriet long desired to create a piece representing "palatial portals." She used the classical themes of earth, air, and water in her conception of the 17-foot high Golden Gates, which were to be cast in bronze and gilded to look like gold.[24] When Harriet was asked to exhibit at the Philadelphia centennial she made plans to send a plaster model of the gates, gilded to look like the original. But in 1876, when she prepared to ship the piece that she had worked on all winter, the central portion was too tall to fit into the hold of the ship. With no time to do anything more elaborate, she sent only a small plaster figure.[25] The commission was awarded elsewhere and the full design was never done in marble.

Another piece that was never completed in marble was the *Sentinel of Pompeii*. Harriet brought the plaster model to London in 1878, and it was one of her few original works after 1870 to attract much attention. Chosen for the subject was an actual Roman sentry, buried alive in the volcanic ash and lava of Vesuvius, refusing to flee the imminent danger. His bones and armor were found at his guard post during a 1794 excavation;

his breastplate, helmet, and lance were moved to the Bourbon Museum in Naples, where the artist studied them.

---

[1] Carr, HH L&M, 15.

[2] Erin Sutherland, *Spotlight Series*, June 2008

[3] Sherwood, 82.

[4] Martinez, *Sister Arts & Artists*, 6.

[5] Carr, HH L&M, 24.

[6] Ibid, 42.

[7] Ibid, 79.

[8] Culkin, 1.

[9] Ibid, 52.

[10] Carr, HH L&M, 136.

[11] Culkin, 61.

[12] Untitled clipping, *The Saturday Evening Gazette*, March 26, 1865, Harriet Hosmer Papers, Watertown Public Library, Watertown, MA.

[13] Backstrom, *Houston Peace News*, 3.

[14] Culkin, 67.

[15] Carr, HH L&M, 183.

[16] Culkin, 70.

[17] Carr, HH L&M, 209.

[18] Jody Culkin and Kate Culkin, *Fauns & Shackles: Homage of Harriet Hosmer 1830-1908)*, Exposition March 18-April 26, 2006, Curated by Kathleen Goncharov.

[19] Sherwood, 310.

[20] Ibid, 262.

[21] George McCue, *Sculpture City St. Louis: Public Sculpture in the Gateway to the West*, (New York: Hudson Hills Press, 1988), 41.

[22] *NY Times*, July 14, 1912

[23] Sherwood, 325.

[24] Ibid, 310.

[25] Ibid, 311.

10

✳

LIFE IN MATURITY

In 1870 the process of unification that had been unfolding in Italy for decades began to fundamentally change the lifestyle of American artists living in Rome. On September 20, 1870, Italian troops entered the city. Pope Pius IX quickly condemned what he saw as an invasion, excommunicating Victor Emmanuel II, the king of Italy. When the Italian army entered Rome, the adventurous artist admitted that she rushed out, "spy glass in hand," but was brought to her senses when "a shell burst within a stone's throw of me and a piece fell not two yards from my feet."[1]

As interest in the neo-classical art form faded, and realism began to take hold after the Civil War, Harriet's popularity began to wane. Rediscovering herself as a writer and an inventor, she produced little sculpture after 1885. She spent most of her time in England, visiting friends, giving an occasional lecture, creating commissioned portraits for various members of royalty, and pursuing other artistic and creative interests.

Harriet returned to the United States in 1888. Though it had been twenty years since her last visit, she was warmly welcomed home. One article raved, "Her life of art and world-wide fame and distinguished associations has left her as simple and unaffected as a child, and the eager energy of the New England girl still characterizes the famous woman."[2]

Still an adventurer, Harriet spent the summer in Maine, then traveled around the country promoting herself and her work through public appearances. She gave two art presentations in Denver, where she was greeted by the governor's wife and given shares in a gold mine. She also took a train trip through the Rockies. Harriet then moved to Chicago for a time, to complete the statue *Isabella of Castille*, her final major work.

Harriet took a more public stance on political issues for women during this time. She developed a relationship with Susan B. Anthony, who in 1889 expressed her hope that Hosmer would form an auxiliary to the National Council of Women for female artists.[3] By 1890, Harriet was lobbying actively for the vote. One paper reported that Harriet, in a speech on female suffrage to the Chicago Women's Club, said "it mattered little which country had it first, but she hoped it might be her own, that it might be the proud privilege of the United States to remove the political disabilities of women."[4] Harriet wouldn't see her hope fulfilled. Women were not granted the right to vote until twelve years after her death.

In 1895, the *Boston Globe* reported on a reception held in honor of Harriet Hosmer in her hometown of Watertown. "Miss

Hosmer was gowned in characteristic costume of blue brocade adorned with the medals which she has won by her work, including the medal of the Order of Merit of Russia, the medal of the King of Bavaria, the Italian medal of the Order of Merit, and the medal awarded her by the Grand Duchess of Russia."[5]

Congruent with her forth-right manner, the 65-year-old Harriet did not hesitate to talk about her youth in Watertown, saying:

"I cannot fail to appreciate the courtesy you have shown me today, but as I stand here the days are brought back to my mind when I was not considered an ornament to society."[6]

"I have been many times asked about my girlhood days in Watertown and the mad pranks I used to play," she continued. "I have been asked if it was true that I was expelled from school, if I was nearly killed on a hand-car, which I started myself; if I was nearly drowned in Fresh Pond in my own sailboat, if I really climbed through the great wooden columns which stand in front of the Town Hall, getting through by that sheer pluck which has carried me through life. To all these I answer yes."[7]

"I have been led by my destiny far from home, and for more than forty years have lived on foreign shores; but each year the old home becomes more dear to me, and I become more and more convinced that the place where one is born is the only place one can really love."[8]

During the time she spent in Chicago, Harriet often visited her cousin, Sarah J. Fuller of Terre Haute, Indiana, the daughter of Hiram Hosmer's sister Isabella. When Sarah's husband, Charles, died in 1896, Harriet moved to Terre Haute to live with her widowed cousin. In March 1898, Hosmer was made an honorary member of the Woman's Department Club of Terre Haute. Harriet gave the organization one of the five casts of Brownings' Hands.

Vivacious and youthful looking well into her sixties, Harriet continued to learn and create, thinking of herself as an inventor for the final years of her life. The late nineteenth century saw fascinating advancements in science and technology, creating numerous new interests for Harriet. She looked forward to the day of the airship, when "it would be possible to breakfast in America on Monday morning and lunch in England early the next day."[9] She pursued patents for synthetic marble, a permanent magnet, and a mechanical sheet music page-turning device for musicians. She also proposed a never-built ride for the 1893 World's Columbian Exposition that would simulate space travel. The design included an enormous tower, topped by a glowing glass sphere to represent the sun, around which a series of passenger cars would orbit, representing the planets.

Harriet devoted much of her final thirty years to creation of a perpetual motion machine. This obsession with perpetual motion was closely tied to her belief in Spiritualism, as both rested on the ability to harness powerful unseen forces. Harriet was convinced that lasting fame would come to her through this invention.

While in Terre Haute, Harriet began to write a memoir. The

manuscript titled "Fate and I" was never finished.[10]

In 1899, at the age of 69, Harriet returned to her hometown of Watertown. She enjoyed reminiscing, telling stories about her life. Cornelia Carr wrote: "Those who were so fortunate as to be present when she was in one of those moods, delighted still more in listening to her brilliant sketches of character, personality, genius, wit, and humor. The last, perhaps, made the most vivid impression upon her, because of her own fun-loving nature. To her all life was sunshine, even the clouds were golden and rose-hued, yet beneath all this lived an earnest spirit and lofty determination to do her best and to see only the best in others. Her grateful, loyal, and generous nature drew from others of their highest, making her very presence a benediction."[11]

In her final months, she dreamed of her death, telling Cornelia how she insisted in the dream that her monument be of yellow marble "because it harmonized with my complexion."[12]

Harriet Hosmer "passed into the Higher Life…her mind undimmed"[13] at the age of 77, on February 21, 1908. *The Boston Globe* titled her obituary, "Most Famous of American Women Sculptors,"[14] while at least one obituary expressed surprise that she was still alive. Harriet's body was cremated, her ashes buried alongside her parents and siblings in Mount Auburn Cemetery.

A visionary spirit, the work she dreamed of would easily have filled another lifetime.

[1] Culkin, 112.

[2] Ibid, 136.

[3] Ibid, 141.

[4] Ibid.

[5] *The New York Times*, September 23, 1895.

[6] Ibid.

[7] Ibid.

[8] Ibid.

[9] Sherwood, 329.

[10] Culkin,162.

[11] Carr, HH L&M, 356.

[12] Sherwood, 329.

[13] Ibid, 330.

[14] Culkin, 1.

11

✳

THE INFLUENCE
OF SPIRITUALISM

Harriet's personal quest to understand life after death greatly influenced the course of her career. Her deep interest in "life beyond the veil" and her "gift of second sight"[1] led her to an exploration of Spiritualism, a religion enjoying a swift rise in popularity during her lifetime. It was said that women played an important part in the rapid spread of this new belief system because they were considered to be more responsive to spiritual influences than men.

Central to this faith was the practice of conversing with the deceased through a medium. Believers thought that communication with departed ancestors and loved ones would bring greater wisdom and understanding to life, creating social change on an individual as well universal level.

100 | B<small>LAZING A</small> T<small>RAIL</small>

Other tenets of Spiritualist philosophy include:

- A belief in a Divine Energy that exists within and around everything.
- The idea that individuals create their own happiness or unhappiness as they obey or disobey Nature's physical and spiritual laws.
- The concept that each person is given enormous potential that can be used to improve their life and the lives of others.

Spiritualists also put great emphasis on the Golden Rule: "Do unto others as you would have them do unto you."

The followers of Spiritualism saw a need to bring forth a new concept of religion—"one that need not be mired in dogma formulated in distant times and places." They felt that, instead, religion could "be progressive, imparting celestial wisdom more or less continuously to those in need."[2]

This perspective fit with Harriet's viewpoint that there was much more to life, just outside of human view. Like the religious and cultural reformers of her time, Harriet held the conviction that the secrets of the spiritual world were not impenetrable, and important new information would soon be revealed.

In this belief system, matter and spirit were seen as intertwined, contrary to the separation of mind and body that had been the dominant thought in Western philosophy. Because of this connection, it was believed that a person could look at human life to understand spiritual life, and vice versa. In essence, Harriet, and those who shared her beliefs, asserted that the principles that governed the material world were the same as those that operated in the spiritual realm. The same concept is expressed in current metaphysical thought: As above so below, as below so above.

Writer and researcher Charles Colbert concluded that many Americans turned to Spiritualism because they could not accept the idea of infant damnation propounded by Calvinism. The new faith abandoned this fearful concept, claiming that children at death were immediately sent to paradise, where they would continue to grow and develop. This had to be a belief that resonated deeply with Harriet as she considered the loss of her young siblings.

It is not known for certain whether or not Harriet had experiences that connected her with the deceased members of her family, but it was written that throughout her life she was subject to visions and communications from the world beyond.[3]

This was an area of interest and study, as well as a life philosophy that Harriet and many of her closest friends shared. Professor McDowell, who taught Harriet anatomy in St. Louis, was known to have a strong belief in spiritualism, believing that the anatomy of the human body held "the vital fluid of the soul."[4] It was said that he experienced several ghostly encounters and devoted a significant amount of time to devising experiments to test the validity of psychic phenomena.[5]

Lydia Marie Child also shared this interest in the supernatural. She considered Harriet clairvoyant—able to see a figure "hidden in the shapeless mass of marble."[6] Harriet told of a strange experience the night they first met. Walking home, she said, she "lagged behind to see the moon and stars and to have a good think."[7] She said that she saw a long, thin rail of fence rise up and move to a spot several yards distant, where it remained upright. She later insisted to Cornelia that the incident was not "a joke, but a solemn fact, in which light I most religiously view it."[8]

In Rome, Harriet was part of a British and American circle that gathered to summon the dead from the world beyond. Elizabeth Barrett Browning, also among those who attended, said that Harriet had "visions" and was a "writing medium."[9]

When once questioned about her psychical experiences, Harriet told of several incidents, including one that involved her maid, Rosa:

> *"When I was living in Rome I had for several years a maid named Rosa, to whom I became much attached. She was faithful and competent, and I was greatly distressed when she became ill with consumption and had to leave me. I used to call frequently to see her when I took my customary exercise on horseback, and on one occasion she expressed a desire for a certain kind of wine. I told her I would bring it to her the next morning. This was toward evening, and she appeared no worse than for some days; indeed, I thought her much brighter, and left her with the expectation of calling to see her many times. During the rest of the afternoon I was busy in my studio, and do not remember that Rosa was in my thoughts after I parted from her. I retired to bed in good health and in*

a quiet frame of mind. I always sleep with my doors locked, and in my bedroom in Rome there were two doors; the key to one my maid kept, and the other was turned on the inside. A tall screen stood around my bed. I awoke early the morning after my visit to Rosa and heard the clock in the library next, distinctly strike five, and just then I was conscious of some presence in the room, back of the screen. I asked if any one was there, when Rosa appeared in front of the screen and said, "Adesso sono content, adesso sono felice' (Now I am content, now I am happy). For the moment it did not seem strange, I felt as though everything was as it had been. She had been in the habit of coming into my room early in the morning. In a flash she was gone. I sprang out of bed. There was no Rosa there. I moved the curtain, thinking that she might have playfully hidden behind its folds. The same feeling induced me to look into the closet. The sight of her had come so suddenly, that in the first moment of surprise and bewilderment I did not reflect that the door was locked. When I became convinced that there was no one in the room but myself, I recollected that fact, and then I thought I must have seen a vision.

After breakfast I mentioned the apparition to my French landlady, and she ridiculed the idea as being anything more than the fantasy of an excited brain. To me it was a distinct fact, and is to this day a distinct vision. Instead of going to see Rosa after breakfast, I sent to enquire, for I felt a strong premonition that she was dead. The messenger returned saying

Rosa had died at five o'clock....To me this occurrence is as much of a reality as any experience in my life."[10]

In another clairvoyant experience, Harriet woke from "forty winks" on the sofa with a sense of a carriage accident. Ten minutes later there was a tremendous crash under her windows. "Up I flew to the nearest window and there was the Princess Orsini's carriage, upside down." Summarizing the incident, Harriet said, "So you see what a witch I am!"[11]

Harriet also told of many times she experienced strange flashes of inner vision, seeing items that she or her companions had lost that she was then quickly able to find.

According to Elizabeth Barrett Browning, *Puck* was inspired by an encounter Harriet had with the spirit of a child. She said that as Hosmer was "entering her bedroom one evening, a spirit, some three feet high, exquisitely formed, came running, dancing to her from the furthest end of the room close up to her knees, and when she stooped towards it, it vanished."[12]

A clue suggesting that *Will o'the Wisp* may have been inspired in a similar way appears is a poem written by an admirer praising Hosmer's "clairvoyant eye [that] doth see Will-o-the-Wisp by tarn and tree."[13]

Harriet remarked that though she did not know the precise source of her visions, she was sure it would "be made clear sometime, perhaps not at any distant day."[14] She was confident that the scientific developments of the time would be able to explain much of what had previously been seen as wondrous phenomena. She argued that her ability to sense unseen events was not supernatural but was related to some "natural law by which things invisible to the human eye may be projected on the mental screen."[15] The idea, she explained, was no wilder than the magic of the photograph.

Some idea of her expectations of the future can be culled from a play she wrote, "1975 A Prophetic Drama." It is the story of two Englishmen, mysteriously mummified in 1875, coming to life in a British Museum a century later to discuss the developments of the past hundred years. One character, speaking of electricity, explains that in the earlier era, "the manipulators of that mysterious agent had already appeared. They were called mediums, but it was left for the twentieth century to understand to utilize their particular gifts."[16] The play concludes by reproving the audience for denying the existence of what it did not understand. The only impediments to progress, in Harriet's eyes, were those created "by a mind unwilling to confront its own vast potential."[17]

In the future that Harriet divined, machines would endow everyone with powers that were then only intuitively and intermittently practiced, and the telepathic powers she shared with her intimates would become commonplace.[18]

"A spiritualist to the end, Harriet would have been thrilled with her life after death."[19]

[1] Sherwood, 40.

[2] Colbert, 29.

[3] Ibid.

[4] Colbert, 30.

[5] Ibid.

[6] Sherwood, 37.

[7] Ibid, 38.

[8] Carr, HH L&M, 14.

[9] Sherwood, 91.

[10] Carr, HH L&M, 128-129.

[11] Sherwood, 249.

[12] Ibid.

[13] Colbert, 37.

[14] Ibid, 34.

[15] Sherwood, 38.

[16] Culkin, 123.

[17] Colbert, 46.

[18] Ibid, 47.

[19] Culkin, Kate, 167.

12

✳

RELATIONSHIPS &
SEXUAL ORIENTATION

In the late 1800s women were still treated as second-class citizens. They were not encouraged to obtain a real education or pursue a professional career. They did not have a public voice and would not be given the right to vote for many years to come. They were expected to restrict their sphere to their home and family.

While Harriet's education at Mrs. Sedgewick's took place when the constraints on women were beginning to be openly questioned, marriage remained the sole aim of a woman's existence as defined by social norms. It was a serious step, nearly irrevocable except by death—seen by young women as a moment when the laughter and play of youth must end, and duty to a husband begin. After marriage, women did not have the right to own their own property, keep their own wages, or sign a contract.

Though it was a step that all young women were expected to take, many expressed misgivings when they observed the social restraints and barriers that came with marriage.

A statement in the *Saturday Review* best summed up the dominant social view: "An unmarried woman is only half a woman, and therefore can only deliver half truths."[1] Reformer Frances Power Cobbe responded, addressing the severely constricting gender lines that limited women's education, health, and character:

"It is as absurd to try to keep a woman feminine in mind by making her learn French because a man learns Latin, as it would be to keep her so in person by making her eat mutton because a man eats beef! Endless are the absurdities of this kind extant among us. Men ought to be well-informed: let women, then, know nothing.... Men ought to be strong and healthy: let a woman's cheek...display the charming morbidezza of partial disease....Not, however, by narrowing and clipping every faculty, not by pinching her in mental stays shall we make a true woman. Such processes produce Dolls, not Women."[2]

Speaking out on behalf of Hatty's strong personality, Mrs. Child once said, "Here was a woman who, at the very outset of her life, refused to have her feet cramped by the little Chinese shoes, which society places on all us [women], and then misnames our feeble tottering feminine grace."[3]

When Harriet returned home to Watertown after studying in St. Louis, she knew her next choices would have a profound impact on her life. She saw her path beginning to diverge from those of her school friends, and she expressed a genuine fear of separation as they began to marry and have children.

When her dear friend Cornelia Crow made plans to marry Lucien Carr in the spring of 1853, Harriet wrote her a letter sharing her thoughts about equality in relationship. "Aim at that 'golden mean' which will lead you to preserve harmony and good feeling without offending your own sense of self-respect. A husband who rules a wife is in my opinion quite as contemptible as a woman who rules a husband. It was never intended that a wife should *obey* a husband for that is the duty of a child toward a parent, but a husband is a friend, a companion and should be an equal."[4]

For herself, Harriet knew that she would need to choose between art and a conventional life that would include marriage. She did not feel she could have both. "Even if so inclined, an artist has no business to marry. For a man, it may be well enough, but for a woman, on whom matrimonial duties and care weigh more heavily, it is a moral wrong, I think, for she must neglect her profession or her family, becoming neither a good wife and mother nor a good artist. My ambition is to become the latter...."[5]

The decision to become an artist rather than a wife left Harriet in a social no-man's land. She began to form relationships with other independent women, a pattern of sisterhood first experienced with the other adolescent females at Mrs. Sedgwick's.

This was not unusual. In the nineteenth century, women's strong, intimate relationships with each other were viewed as normal. The tradition of women's friendships was passed on from one generation to the next, mother to daughter, as a safeguard against loneliness and alienation.[6] Many were relationships born of the need for comfort and support, and involved married as well as single women. Society recognized that a husband could not always be counted on for the closeness and emotional support extended by one woman to another.

Most of these relationships stemmed from the basic need to reach out to another human being. Within the social and cultural milieu of the time, it was not easy for unmarried women to form close relationships with men unless those males were fathers or brothers or otherwise related.

It was a "world of female intimacy" where closeness, both physical and emotional, was not taboo.[7] Historians of sexuality have written extensively about the nature of these partnerships and debated how to understand them and how to refer to them. Some use the term "lesbian," while others say that this projects a modern understanding of sexuality onto the past. How can we define "lesbian" in a historical moment in which this terminology was unknown and perhaps even unthought?[8]

Harriet Hosmer never married. She was known to have deep friendships with both men and women. Whether or not any of these relationships were sexual is a source of debate. In Rome, Harriet found social freedom unheard of in America and a group of other independent young people to share it with.

Cobbe wrote enthusiastically of the "happy way women club together in Italy," reveling in the evidence that women could be "cheerful, independent professionals without enduring stoic discomfort or constricted social lives. There was a brightness, freedom, and joyousness among these gifted Americans which was delightful to me."[9]

Harriet's friendship with sculptor Shakspere Wood can perhaps be seen as one of her closest intimate and potentially romantic friendships with a male of her own age. She was seen often enough alone in his company to cause comment. Her friends at one point conjectured whether rumors about his getting married might be "with Hatty herself."[10]

The "very good looking" Sir Frederic Leighton, then young and untitled, was another male with whom Harriet had a frank and cordial friendship that ended only with his death.[11]

Harriet also had many close female relationships. She referred to Cornelia as her "dear sister" and also expressed jealousy toward Lucien Carr. When she first moved to Rome she lived in the household of Cornelia Carr, whose sexual orientation has been the source of much discussion.

Despite the conjecture, Harriet asserted her celibate status in a letter to Wayman Crow in 1854, writing, "I am the only faithful worshipper of Celibacy, and her service becomes more fascinating the longer I remain in it."[12] Hatty's single status was a recurring theme in their communication over the years, sometimes serious, sometimes comic. "I have been searching vainly for Mr. Hosmer," she told him once, but decided, "I must leave it to sharper eyes than my own to find him."[13]

She also joked about being a spinster with her friend Anne Dundas, writing, "By the way, I hear there is a letter waiting for me at the Poste Restante. Would it bore you too much to bring it along with you? It may be an offer of marriage for all I know, and those chances come far too seldom to neglect any!"[14]

Cobbe's essay, "Celibacy vs. Marriage," presented a picture of the single life that fit well with Harriet's character, and, most likely, her experience. "The old maid of 1861," she wrote, "is an exceedingly cheery personage, running about untrammelled by husband or children," and she is "far more independently happy than a single man because she can make true and tender friendships, such as not one man's heart in a hundred can imagine."[15]

Harriet filled her life with heartfelt, fun, and long-lasting friendships. She also often referred to her "flirtations," a word that captures the playful, romantic, and transitory nature of some of these relationships.

When Harriet met Lady Louisa Ashburton in 1867, her concept of relationship took a more serious turn. Harriet recalled "becoming transfixed" at first sight, the day the Scottish woman appeared in her studio. She described Louisa's classic beauty, "humanized by a pair of keen, dark eyes, a radiant smile, and a rich, vibrant voice."[16] In her letters, Harriet sometimes spoke of herself as Ashburton's "hubby," referring to Louisa as her "beloved" or "my sposa." The relationship endured for decades, even though the two were often separated for long periods of time. Harriet returned to England when Maysie, Lady Ashburton's daughter, died in 1902. When Louisa herself died a few months later, Harriet was at her side.

---

[1] Sally Mitchell, Frances Power Cobb: Victorian Feminist, Journalist, Reformer (University of Virginia Press, 2004), 127.

[2] Ibid.

[3] Sherwood, 13.

[4] Sherwood, 104.

[5] Carr, HH L&M, 35.

[6] Sherwood, 41.

[7] Ibid, 20.

[8] Lisa Merrill, When Rome Was a Woman (University of Michigan Press, 2000), xi.

[9] Mitchell, 123.

[10] Sherwood, 118.

[11] New York Times, July 14, 1912

[12] Carr, HH L&M, 35.

[13] Sherwood, 170.

[14] Ibid, 211.

[15] Mitchell,126.

[16] Sherwood, 265.

"I honor all those who step boldly forward, and in spite of ridicule and criticism, pave a broader way for the women of the next generation."

Epilogue

Harriet Goodhue Hosmer, lived life at full capacity. Her travels spanned the continents, while her way of life and influential presence traversed huge barriers that defined and limited acceptable behavior. Like others who have led the way into uncharted territory, she was opposed, ridiculed, and misunderstood. Yet she refused to accept societal constraints and courageously stood strong in what she believed was the right path for her.

In a letter written to the Reverend Phebe A. Hanaford, one of the first clergywomen in America, Harriet shares, in her typically positive manner, her own attitude toward the criticism and scorn she experienced:

"What a country mine is for women! Here every woman has a chance, if she is bold enough to avail herself of it; and I am proud of every woman who is bold enough. I honor every woman who has strength enough to step out of the beaten path

*when she feels that her walk lies in another–strength enough
to stand up and be laughed at if necessary.... In a few years
it will not be thought strange that women should be preachers
and sculptors, and everyone who comes after us will have to
bear fewer and fewer blows. Therefore I say, I honor all those
who step boldly forward, and in spite of ridicule and criticism,
pave a broader way for the women of the next generation."* [1]

The challenges Harriet Hosmer would overcome, the impact
of her life, and the depth of her character were clearly foreseen
by her anatomy professor, J. N. McDowell. In a letter written in
August 1858, fifty years before her death, he said:

*"To see a man mount step by step through difficulties,
and at last stand on the first round of fame's proud ladder,
commands admiration. But to see a woman dare to scale the
mountain height of fame, when she has the heroic courage to
plant her ladder on a precipice and lean it on a storm cloud,
and dare the lightning's angry passion of jealousy, makes the
generous bosom heave with love for the sex and glory that we
were born of woman.... May the snowy peak of the mount of
Miss Hosmer's glory ever stand as a beacon to woman's daring.
Her heart was as pure as the untrodden mountain snowflake,
and her footsteps were as firm as its eternal foundation."* [2]

---

[1] Petersen & Wilson, 80.

[2] Carr, HH L&M, 126.

✳

MOUNT HOSMER TODAY

"By day and by night, winter and summer, no matter what may befall the fortunes of Lansing, regardless of high water or a falling river, Mount Hosmer stands, a buttress and protection, almost a symbol of the security and dignity of this historic old river town." [1]

Over 150 years since its' naming, Mount Hosmer continues to attract the attention of visitors to this corner of northeast Iowa. Famous for offering breathtaking views of three states: Iowa, Minnesota, and Wisconsin, the lookouts on Mount Hosmer offer a spectacular panorama of fifty miles of the beautiful Mississippi River valley. Situated above the National Fish & Wildlife Refuge, with the historic Black Hawk Bridge in the foreground and overlooking the sharpest curve of the river, the site is a favorite for sightseers and photographers.

The hill was originally donated to the Lansing American Legion Post in 1920. The Post established a memorial to

Allamakee County veterans in 1922, planting 634 white pine trees to represent each county resident who had fought in World War I. Just a few years later, in 1925, most of these trees were destroyed in a fire, and in 1926 the property was donated to the city of Lansing. The city dedicated the land as Veterans Memorial Park in 1928.

That same year flagpoles and memorial tablets were placed on three overlook points on Mount Hosmer in memory of three Lansing soldiers who lost their lives in WWI. These soldiers and their original memorial tablets are:

BECK POINT, overlooking the Mississippi River. Dedicated to the memory of William E. Beck, who died in World War I at Fismes, battle of Aisnes-Marine, August 4, 1918.

STRONG POINT, overlooking the center of town. Dedicated to the memory of Robert Strong, who was killed in World War I, battle of the Meuse-Argonne, October 2, 1918.

GYLNN POINT, overlooking the west end of town. Dedicated to the memory of George R. Glynn, who died in World War I at Boise de Gesme, battle of the Meuse-Argonne, October 5, 1918.

Flags continue to fly from these poles today.

The Lansing American Legion and VFW Posts rededicated the memorial on Veterans Day, November 11, 2001, placing three limestone boulders, each with a plaque telling history of the site. Behind the boulders is a semi-circle of six white pine trees, planted as a symbolic replacement of the trees destroyed by fire.

Another special tree stands on the center knoll where the road diverges at the top of the hill. A stone marker identifies a Mt. Vernon Walnut, one of 48 planted, one in each state, commemorating the Washington Bicentennial in 1962.

In addition to the memorial, the land atop the wooded bluff has been developed into a 104-acre city park with lookout points, telescopes, hiking trails, a shelter, picnic areas, and playground equipment.

Driving up the narrow road to the park is an adventure in its own right, the entrance opening to what has been described as the sharpest corner with the steepest grade in Iowa.

A plaque explaining how the park got its name is posted near the upper lookout.

---

[1] "Old Mount Hosmer," *The Book of the Black Hawk Bridge*, (1931), 21.

$$\text{✳}$$

Appendix A

The following is a listing of Harriet Goodhue Hosmer's major works, as well as their current locations*:

• *Hesper, the Evening Star*, 1852, Watertown Free Public Library, Watertown, Mass.

• *The Clasped Hands of Robert Browning and Elizabeth Barrett Browning*, 1853, The New York Metropolitan Museum of Art, New York, N.Y.; Armstrong-Browning Library, Baylor University, Waco, Texas; Boston Public Library, Boston, Mass.; Newark Museum, Newark, N.J.; St. Louis Art Museum, St. Louis, Mo.; Wellesley College, Wellesley, Mass.; Schlesinger Library, Harvard University, Cambridge, Mass.; National Museum of Women in the Arts, Washington, D.C.; National Portrait Gallery, London, England; National Gallery of Art, Washington, D.C.

• *Daphne*, 1854, The Metropolitan Museum of Art, New York, N.Y.

• *Medusa*, 1854, Detroit Institute of Arts, Detroit, Mich.; Minneapolis Institute of the Arts, Minneapolis, Minn.; Hood Art Museum, Dartmouth College, Dartmouth, N.H.

• *Oenone*, 1855, Mildred Lane Kemper Art Museum, St. Louis, Mo.

• *Puck*, 1856, Chrysler Museum of Art, Norfolk, Va.; Smithsonian American Art Museum, Washington, D.C.; Watertown Free Public Library, Watertown, Mass.; Lenox Library Association, Lenox, Mass.; Art Gallery of New South Wales, Sydney, Australia; Senate Chambers of Barbados, Bridgetown, Barbados; Walker Art Center, Liverpool, England; Borough Museum, Kendal, England; The Huntington Library, Art Collections, and Botanical Gardens, San Marino, Calif.; Forest Hills Cemetery and the Forest Hills Educational Trust, Boston, Mass.; Dr. and Mrs. William H. Gerdts, New York, N.Y.

• *Will-O-the-Wisp*, 1856, 1858, 1864, Chrysler Museum, Norfolk, Va.; Smithsonian Art Museum, Washington, D.C.; Watertown Free Public Library, Watertown, Mass.; Second Variation: Boston Athenaeum, Boston, Mass.; Third Variation: Chrysler Museum, Norfolk, Va.

• *Beatrice Cenci*, 1856-1857, St. Louis Mercantile Library, St. Louis, Mo; Art Gallery of New South Wales, Sydney, Australia.

• *Tomb of Judith Falconnet*, 1858, Church of Sant'Andrea della Fratte, Rome.

• *Zenobia in Chains*, 1859, Huntington Library, Art Collections, and Botanical Gardens, San Marino, Calif.; Wadsworth Athenaeum, Hartford, Conn.; St. Louis Museum of Fine Arts, St. Louis, Mo.; Art Institute of Chicago, Chicago, Ill.; Watertown Free Public Library, Watertown, Mass.

• *Thomas Hart Benton*, 1862 (dedicated 1868), Lafayette Park, St. Louis, Mo.

• *Sleeping Faun*, 1865, Department of Foreign Affairs, Dublin, Ireland; Cleveland Museum of Art, Cleveland, Ohio; Museum of Fine Arts, Boston, Mass.

• *Waking Faun*, 1866, unknown, thought to be destroyed.

• *Portrait of Wayman Crow*, 1866, Washington University Gallery of Art, St. Louis, Mo.; Watertown Free Public Library, Watertown, Mass.

• *Queen of Naples*, 1868, unknown.

• *African Sibyl*, 1888-1896, unknown, thought to be destroyed.

• *Fountain of the Mermaid's Cradle*, 1892-1893, Fountain Square, Flint Park, Larchmont, N.Y.

• *Queen Isabella*, 1893, unknown, thought to be destroyed.

* Adapted from the work of Patricia Cronin: *Harriet Hosmer, Lost & Found*, 2009, and verified to the best of my ability.

＊

REFERENCES

Backstrom, Jane: Houston Peace News, *Harriet Hosmer, Feminist Sculptor.* February 1994, p. 3.

Botkin, B.A., ed., *A Treasury of Mississippi River Folklore,* New York: American Legacy Press, 1955.

Burke, William J.: *The Upper Mississippi Valley: How the Landscape Shaped Our Heritage,* Waukon, Iowa: Mississippi Valley Press, 2000.

"Bridging the past with the future," *Lansing Fish Days Commemorative Book 2000.* Prairie du Chien, Wisc.: Howe Printing Company.

Chadwick, Patricia, *"Harriet Hosmer Biography-American Sculptor,"* http://txtx.assortment.com/harriethosmera_rafd.htm, (accessed August 5, 2003).

Colbert, Charles: *Harriet Hosmer & Spiritualism,* American Art, Volume 10, No. 3, Autumn 1996, pp. 28-49.

Colbert, Charles: *Haunted Visions: Spiritualism & American Art,* Philadephia: University of Pennsylvania Press, 2011.

Cronin, Patricia: *Harriet Hosmer, Lost and Found,* Charta Books, LTD, 2009.

Culkin, Jody, and Culkin, Kate: *Fauns and Shackles: Homage of Harriet Hosmer (1830-1908)*, Exposition March 18-April 26, 2006, curated by Kathleen Goncharov.

Culkin, Kate: *Harriet Hosmer: A Cultural Biography,* Amherst and Boston: University of Massachusetts Press, 2010.

Dunstan, Angela: *"Nineteenth-Century Sculpture and the Imprint of Authenticity."*

Hancock, Ellery M.: *Past and Present of Allamakee County, Volume I, Illustrated,* Chicago, S.J. Clarke Publishing Co., 1913.

Havighurst, Walter: *Upper Mississippi, A Wilderness Saga.* New York: Rinehart & Co., 1944.

Hosmer, Harriet Goodhue and Carr, Cornelia: *Harriet Hosmer: Letters and Memories.* Moffat, Yard, and Company, reprint of 1912 edition.

Lansing Iowa on the Mississippi, 1867-1967, Centennial booklet, 1967.

Leach, Joseph: *Bright Particular Star: The Life and Times of Charlotte Cushman,* www.cardinalbook.com/fmorcush.htm

Marshall, Gail: *Harriet Hosmer and the Classical Inheritance.* Court of the University of St. Andrews, 2003, Vol. xxxix, No. 2, 202-213.

Martinez, Michele: *Sister Arts and Artists: Elizabeth Barrett Browning's Aurora Leigh and the Life of Harriet Hosmer.* Court of the University of St. Andrews, 2008.

Merrill, Lisa: *When Rome Was a Woman.* University of Michigan Press, 2000.

Mitchell, Sally: *Frances Power Cobbe: Victorian Feminist, Journalist, Reformer.* University of Virginia Press, 2004.

New York Times, from the Boston Globe: "Harriet Hosmer in her Native Town," September 23, 1895.

New York Times: "Woman As Artist," July 14, 1912.

Oles, Carole Simmons, *Waking Stone: Inventions on the Life of Harriet Hosmer,* Fayetteville: The University of Arkansas Press, 2006.

Peterson, Karen and Wilson, J.J.: *Women Artists: Recognition & Reappraisal From the Early Middle Ages to the Twentieth Century.* Harper Colophon Books, 1976, pp. 79-84.

Sherwood, Dolly: *Harriet Hosmer: American Sculptor 1830-1908.* University of Missouri Press, 1991.

Terre Haute newspaper: "Wabash Valley Profiles," April 7, 2002.

The Palimpsest. Iowa City: The State Historical Society of Iowa, October, 1966.

Tousley, Albert S., ed., *The Book of the Black Hawk Bridge*, Lansing, Iowa: The Tepee Press, 1931.

Tousley, Albert S., *Where the River Goes*, Iowa City, Iowa: The Tepee Press, 1928.